MW00609869

Thread of Blue

Thread of Blue

A Journey through Loss, Faith, and Renewal

Judy Belsky

TARGUM/FELDHEIM

First published 1992
Second edition 2003
Copyright © 1992, 2003 by Judy Belsky
ISBN 1-56871-251-0

Published by:
TARGUM PRESS, INC.
22700 W. Eleven Mile Rd.
Southfield, MI 48034
E-mail: targum@netvision.net.il
Fax: 888-298-9992
www.targum.com

Distributed by:
FELDHEIM PUBLISHERS
202 Airport Executive Park
Nanuet, NY 10954
www.feldheim.com

Printed in Israel

Contents

Dedication

Ten years have passed since the original printing of *Thread of Blue*. When it was published, there were very few books about grief. Not a popular subject. And *Thread of Blue* is written as a poetic meditation, not in easy prose.

But gradually, *Thread of Blue* began to be requested. Requested by individuals who would approach me and tell me they had lost a young family member. Requested by families in Israel who have suffered loss at the hands of our enemies. Requested by victims of September 11. Requested by synagogue rabbis and chaplains who counsel the bereaved. Requested by people suffering from illness. Requested by people who want to find a way back after loss, any loss.

Thread of Blue slowly unwinds its message and helps knit together the sorrows of its readers.

Someone, outside of me, kept their eye on the slow and steady impact of *Thread of Blue*. Someone cared enough to perpetuate the memory of Yosef through the book; someone cared for the readers who might find strength in it. Someone cared for my writing and encouraged me.

This *Thread of Blue*, with its new format and chapter introductions, is dedicated to my dear brother and sister-in-law David and Victoria Benoliel, who made its production possible and who believed in it from the start. May they be rewarded for their act of kindness and love with the Blessed Lord's kindness and love.

Foreword

by Rebbetzin Sara E. Freifeld

Thread of Blue is a book that embraces the essence of faith. It has the power to awaken, to stir, to transform. Only on the surface is it a book about loss. In all its depths it is a book about Life from the particular intersection known as Death.

The author is a woman of extraordinary spiritual strength. Her journey toward wholeness is a journey we all must take. Loss is a part of all life; yet there are so few people who can teach us to mourn, to reconstruct life after tragedy, to rebuild the broken heart so that it can once more be whole.

Thread of Blue reveals the soul of a Jew who refuses to be exiled by the *hester panim* (God's concealment) of tragedy. Repeatedly, she knocks at the door of the Palace. Insistent, she awaits entry. She yearns for the reunion with the Creator that she knew in times of joy.

Out of her yearning she creates *tefillah*, an offering of her innermost self. It is the dialogue of her soul with the Creator filtered through the language of our Fathers. It takes us from the place of despair to the heights of redemption. As such, *Thread of Blue* transcends the story of one individual and is characteristic of the Jewish experience as a whole. As Jews we move through time and history from brokenness to wholeness, from slavery to redemption, from tragedy to joy. She reminds us that to await redemption with a pure faith is *simchah*.

Thread of Blue is a poetic tapestry of intricate beauty and depth. It is written in a poet's language in order that it reach the place in us that responds to the mystery of words, of holy words that come to rouse the slumbering soul.

This work enlivens our perceptions, cleanses them and honors them. It is the task of one's existence to awaken to the River of Light that flows within each of us. We can do no better than to look toward this book for such an awakening.

৵৽৽৻

Thread of Blue is a slender, firm thread that binds me to my son who died at the age of sixteen in an accident.

There are no accidents. I was meant to give birth to him, to name him in loving memory of my father. I was meant to know the experience of this son, this only son.

I was meant to lose him just at the age when we could see him emerge into independence. We could begin to see what he treasured, what he was made of. At sixteen, we could not yet see the entire structure, but enough of the scaffold to imagine the beauty of the building.

Whatever small tasks he forgot to do, he always remembered to prepare a presentation on the Torah portion. He typed these words and presented them at our Shabbos table clearly and forcefully. Earlier, his rosh hayeshivah had commented about him: the neshamah is in the speech, and his speech is gifted.

I was meant to sense his soul talents, to wait for fruition. I was meant to suffer the disruption of life, the shock of his death.

Death shook me. In the storm, I found out how strong are the bonds of love and friendship. How tight are the bonds to the Holy One. So tight, He never let go of me.

Thread of Blue

Speak to the children of Israel and tell them to make fringes on the corners of their garments throughout their generations and to put on the fringes of the corner a Thread of Blue...[1]

During the *shivah* for my son Yosef, many people came bearing gifts of the heart. One friend sat near us, wrapped up in our agony, remembering losses of his own. He recalled that his Rebbe had said that the white background of the fringes can be likened to one's ordinary reality — the times in life when things flow in a predictable pattern. The Thread of Blue is the shock that bursts onto the other, ordinary pattern of life, utterly changing and disrupting it.

This writing began as a need to acknowledge the Thread of Blue that is the loss of our beloved son. As it grew and assumed process and form, the writing created the imaginary doorway that would open points of access in my exploration of both the terrain of the Thread of Blue and the background white.

Each time I venture forth into the reality of the death a door opens. Through this door I reenter the background white. The deeper I enter the Thread of Blue, the acknowledgment and acceptance of death, the more deeply I begin to reexperience the joys of everyday living.

The freedom to travel between the two terrains has changed my view. The angle of my vision has widened to include a broader range. And now, if the blue is bluer, the white is whiter. To pain and loss I am a sister; to humor and joy a friend.

Along the way I have lost the innocence that can only be the way of the one who is sheltered from suffering and loss. For the innocent, the blue does not fall within their angle of vision; it is as far removed from their perspective as the background white is to the mourner in the initial stage of shock and anguish.

The innocent looks out onto a world that is radically different from mine. The disparity in our views creates a dissonance that overwhelms me. There is a country I used to know, from whose citizenship I am now barred. My experience no longer fits within its boundaries.

At this time, in solitude, the writing helps to sustain the integrity of my view, helps to define the dimensions of my new landscape.

As I persist in this exploration I realize that I am striving to strengthen my connectedness to the *Ribbono shel Olam*, Master of the Universe. In my insistence on delving into my loss instead of detouring from it, I am saying to Him: I do not let You leave me. Be with me wherever I am. Accompany me, let me perceive You even in the depths of bereavement.

In my sense of connectedness, there is a consolation; in my perception of my primary relationship, there is Light. I experience the belief that "there is no sadness in the world to one who recognizes the Light of truth."[2]

It is not that I am finished with sadness, but rather that the quest for connectedness transcends the search for happiness.

❧

A student of my husband's is going to be married. He had grown up in our home. We introduced him to his bride. We were on a shopping trip to outfit the children for the wedding. I suddenly feel weak and want to return home. I cut short the shopping trip.

On the way home, I suddenly recall fragments of a dream I had before awakening that morning. Yosef was injured. He asked me to hold him. He said he had to go on a long trip. I think he said the word journey.

As we enter the house, the phone is ringing.

Before the reality has sunk in, there is a funeral.

Ribbons

We bring God what He has asked.

We form a winding trail of cars on the way to the burial of my son, my only son, who is dead at sixteen. We are a ribbon. The gaps between us are an optical illusion. We are connected, a string of hearts sent together on a mission.

The way is slow and time is gently warped. Is the journey one of hours, minutes, or an eternity? There is no fair measure for this experience by the usual means. This weaving ribbon of humanity exists above time. We are connected to each other and to our source.

To bury the dead is called the Kindness of Truth,[3] "true" because it is free of ulteriority. We can expect no like response from the recipient of our benevolence, since he is dead. In the Kindness of Truth, we move beyond reciprocity, and thus beyond time and space.

The dead send us a ribbon of sheer mitzvah in the purest form we can know in this finite world...they reveal to us a glimpse of Beyond.

We wind slowly, we make many stops and starts in order to remain together along the highway. I notice that we are proceeding to New Jersey. I hear the names of Woodbridge and Floral Park pass between my husband and the driver, our friend. I sense consternation in my husband over these names, but I allow it to fall away. For I am beyond weakness and beyond strength. My usual control converts to surrender. Let the *Ribbono shel Olam* direct us.

To our left, other traffic passes us as we stall and start along the way in our effort to remain together. On the left, first beside us, then behind us, then beside us again weaves a green truck. I glance at the driver. A chassidic Jew in shirtsleeves winding in and out of our ribbon. I guess that he must belong to this group; otherwise why does he keep reappearing along the way? And yet he is not dressed in the usual manner for a burial. It teases my mind for a moment. I muse that he is a friend of my son. Yosef loved people and people were drawn to him. He had a circle of friends who varied widely in age and walks of life. Yosef was not confused by the disguises people wear.

I muse that this unknown chassid in shirtsleeves is a friend of my son who heard about the funeral only in time to rush away from his work in work clothes.

We arrive at the cemetery. When I see the chassid park his truck and join us, I am satisfied that my theory fits — the parentheses close as I turn away.

My husband's cousins, who are *kohanim*, of priestly descent, cushion our arrival as they stand apart at the edges of the burial place.[4] Because they personify holiness, infinite gradations of holiness send their echoes down to me. They escort my son, they bridge his leave-taking from this world and his entry to the next.

Now the opening for the grave is before us. We are shocked by its lonely setting. There are no other graves nearby. My son's grave site appears solitary on the side of the road. There are no words for this sadness. I see my husband stand aside for a few minutes with his brother who had taken responsibility for the arrangements...

Again, I hear the names of Woodbridge and Floral Park. Whatever the gist of these words, I know I must not listen. It is too late, whatever it is. I must give up my son, and this lonely grave site adds an extra weight to our burdened hearts and minds. I don't dare test the limits of strength now. Let it go, let it go, I tell myself.

On the second day of the *shivah* my husband tells me that he has learned from his brother about the mistake over the burial site. "I made the choice to bury our son in Woodbridge," he says, "because it is an older cemetery and somehow less desolate." This message was misunderstood, and the arrangements were made for Floral Park.

"Do you remember the man in the green truck?" We compare notes now on our memory of him. "He had human cargo, an old man who had died in a nursing home without family or friends to bury him."

The caretaker, the man in shirtsleeves, was to take his body to Floral Park where the old man's grave was ready. In the hopes of providing a proper ceremony, the caretaker called the chapel in Brooklyn and was told that a procession had indeed left for Floral Park. But, they told him, it was too late for him to meet our group, too much time had already gone by. The caretaker decided to try, and he overtook us.

As soon as Yosef's burial was over, just after the family members left, he stated his request to the group that remained. The old man was then buried properly with *kavod* by the same group who had buried our son and with the same *kavod* that our son had consistently shown to old people. Since the old man's plot was at Floral Park, this meeting could not have happened unless our message to have Yosef buried in Woodbridge had been misread.

I remember now my sense of curiosity about the driver, my fantasy that he was a kindred spirit of my son... I remember the sense of timelessness I experienced on the journey, the ribbon tying the group together, the ribbon that comes down that ties us to Heaven. I consider the juxtaposition of zeal in performing a mitzvah with physical odds that deem it unlikely.

Against an entire backdrop of the seemingly absurd contingencies of time and space hangs in stark relief the realization of Potential, the mitzvah. My son's life reverberated with acts of kindness; in death his presence was creative. It was as if he reached down for one more mitzvah, a mitzvah of beauty and incalculable magnitude as an old man was escorted from this world.

The usual ribbons that tie us together and give us identity and comfort are torn apart. But now, something of a different texture steals into our broken hearts and offers to begin to heal and knit them together. We are broken but we glimpse Eternity. In the awful disruption of our usual pattern, we see beyond the pattern of finite relationships. We see beyond ourselves.

As I sense the dimensions of time and space that Yosef has transcended, as I grapple with the meaning of Beyond that my son leads me to, I recall that he has always led me. I recall his Birth poem, the one I wrote on the day of his brit milah. I speak to him now in the language of the first poem.

> *I watch you open and close*
> *Your tiny fist.*
> *I laugh out loud*
> *When they weigh you*
> *And measure you*
> *In my laughter*
> *Rings the laughter of Sarah*
> *The shock of recognition*
> *When all the contingencies*
> *Of time and space*
> *Are swept aside*
> *When she is told*
> *that she will have a son*
> *And that the Covenant with Abraham*
> *Will be kept*
> *And will keep us*
> *And spirit will be raised*
> *Over the dominions*

Of time and space again and again
And the Covenant with Abraham
Will be kept
And it will keep us.
Go my son, grow to this.

❦

Inside the child we bear is a neshamah. We nurture the child. We get glimpses of his soul. Because we are busy caring for his needs, because this time of caring is so rich and compelling and lovely, and because we expect it to last, we forget that he is nine-tenths soul.

His journey is a soul journey. Each of us must travel the orbit of our own soul journeys. When the soul of our son leaves us, we realize he was nine-tenths soul. We realize that as well as we knew him, we did not know him. His soul directs him. Now his orbit leans away from us.

As the casket bearing his body is taken to burial, I rest my hand upon it. I want comfort, I want to know him again, I want to touch him, to have him near.

To know him now, I must release him, let him go. To let him go, I must admit how little I know him. I must release him to the utter individuality of his soul.

To know him now, I have to enter on a personal journey. I have to seek Hashem from the depths of my new position. I strain to sense Eternity.

Lech Lecha is always in the singular.

Rachamim

I stand at the grave of my son.

I am working with every fiber of my being. What do I strain toward with such energy? Is it the sum total of my self striving to maintain sanity? Or, is it a primary basic movement toward meaning? It is both; these are one.

In this work I am pulling Toward, not Away from. The entire current of self seeks the *Ribbono shel Olam*. I address myself to him: *Ribbono shel Olam*, WHAT? (not why?) WHAT?

I repeat the thought. I become the thought. I bend myself into the question. My entire being inclines itself into the One Question. I am a flower whose delicate roots rest in the ground, but whose face slants upward to receive the sun.

WHAT?

In the one unified question there is a multitude of questions. I ask them, knowing there is only one question and only one answer...

I try out the variations. WHAT: what is it you expect of me? I am not Sarah the Mother, not Hannah the Mother of seven martyrs. Not noble. Not great. My only son.

WHAT? What will my life be? In a bitter irony my husband will say Kaddish for his only son. I wonder what our life will be.

WHAT? What do You want of me?

WHAT? What is it that You want me to make of this?

The burial is over. The *shurot*, the human rows through which we pass, are formed by the young, fresh-faced boys from the yeshivah. They comfort me as I walk between them. I feel their closeness to my son in their youth and strength. Their mute pain is a fitting tribute to their friend. Their gift to me is a glance, a recognition that I am the Mother of the boy.

As I walk toward the car that will take us home, I am aware of a nameless and enormous set of sensations. Inside me there are primitive waves, internal movements. These words enter my mind and match the primitive sensation of depth I am experiencing: "From the belly of the underworld I call out to you..."[5]

Sobs well up and rip through me as we reach the car. At first the sobs are wordless and then a refrain attaches itself to the awful rhythm: My Yosef, my baby son, my baby.

We return home to be *aveilim*, mourners. The people stream through our house in the days that follow. The traditional messages of *tanchumim*, comfort, remind the anguished that life in this world is a but corridor to the World to Come.[6] Excesses of grief are not intrinsically Jewish because they imply that all is lost, that there is no continuity, that there is no world beyond this one. No spirit everlasting, no life beyond time, no faith.

Traditional reminders of faith continue. They are designed to remind me of that which I knew, but that which might be driven from my understanding in my loss. But, I insist to no one in particular, I have just been touched by God. I have been pulled out of my former state of constricted consciousness. Maybe I went screaming and kicking, but I am nonetheless transformed. I have no son, but I do have faith.

It is not my faith that is broken, I insist, it is my heart. These are two separate tracks, I insist.

I hold two stones, one in each hand. One contains the experience of faith that is mine in the death. The other is my heart and it is broken. Two stones.

I begin to wonder about a point of integration for these two experiences. I hear the voice within me say that the expression of perfect faith is to accept one's *yesurim* with *ahavah*.[7] Can Faith and Love, the work of the heart, be brought together? Two stones.

My mind carries me back to the grave. Back to the One- and Many-Sided Question. I recreate the nameless sensations that followed the burial, the waves, the primitive waves, that shook and transformed me.

Contractions, I shout silently to myself. It was wave upon wave of contractions. Birth pangs. I am stunned. Echoes of my sobs for my infant replay themselves to me.

I delivered a baby into that grave. In the mystical writings, *kever*, grave, is called *rechem*, womb. What deep and lonely search am I engaged in? I am lone explorer. Alone I must seek the meaning of my own experience. "The soul of man is a lamp of God searching the chambers of the womb."[8]

I delivered a baby into that *kever-rechem*. The grave-womb. The *rechem*-womb is made for *rachamim*, compassion. I lay down in the current, in the flow of God's ways. I enter the rhythm of His way *ad d'lo yoda*,[9] until there is no discernible difference between Give and Take.

God is in me. I am a Light formed from His Light. To walk in His Way, I am *rachum* as He is *rachum*,[10] I match my compassion to His. To be *rachum* as He is *rachum*, I summon my deepest receptivity, my feminine passivity. In order to walk in His Ways I create *rachamim*, with no holding back.

I follow along the traces of the *Ribbono shel Olam* in this world. As I give birth to Yosef a second time in variation, "in my flesh...I perceive God."[11]

I feel my two stones, the stone of Faith and the stone of Heart, melt together as they meet on the path toward *ahavah*, perfect love.

❧

Around us stand family and friends. They accompany us to the grave. They observe our needs and try to meet them before we are aware. They notice the children and provide for them. They bring our meals. They sit before us near the floor and prepare a mourner's meal of round, round eggs. In the lull between visitors they sit, resting their hands in ours.

The tzibbur runs to us. Takes time away from other pursuits. Surrounds us like an army of protective soldiers. Pours compassion into us when we are bereft.

The circle of friends is wider than we know. People touched by Yosef's life. People whose lives we have touched without knowing just how. Links of interactions and responses form a strong, wide circle. The links are made of kindness. The beauty of the faces, the love and sustenance reaches us in a silver stream.

Yosef is not just our son, but a son of the entire community. Not just a son, but a student, classmate, friend. His grieving friends turn their faces to us as well. We look upon them with love. We try to soothe their fright and that strange phenomenon of survivor guilt. Every child belongs to the community.

The Godly acts of Godly people bolster us:

The Godly acts of Godly people remind us of God.

When our voices are broken from weeping, they deliver messages of faith and love.

They are sent by God.

The Unknown

*S*hivah.

The week of mourning. I sit on the floor. Two streams. One inside me; one outside me.

Inside, my sensory awareness is over-tuned. My observing mind misses no detail. But the poles of perception turn back on themselves. A small noise and a great noise are equal; a paper falling to the floor creates a crash. Voices alternate whisper-to-roar. Near is far. Time is warped on gentle wave.

Outside me flows a stream of visitors, those who come to fulfill the mitzvah of comforting the mourners.

Hundreds stream in and out through the week. They form one continuous river of humanity. I cannot relate to more than a few who know me well, or who knew my son well.

The rest overwhelm me. I feel their collective strength. They bring me something I cannot name. It is not the familiarity of interpersonal contact, since they do not know me. They are like a river which bends and eddies off in a hundred directions but nonetheless flows intentionally. Forever it flows to its source in some unseen waterway.

The stream of strange visitors are my people, Israel, who transcend themselves in mitzvah as they follow in the way of the Torah, the Water of Life.[12]

A strange woman enters the room. We are silent. We avoid small talk because it is a poor accompaniment to our experience, and because of our resolve to focus on our son and on our grieving. The woman does not speak because she follows the mourning rule that in opening conversation, the mourner has the right of way.

I begin to feel her presence in the room. I begin to feel an energy leave her and reach out to me.

I lift my eyes to her and almost perceptibly raise a hand. I hum to her, all my motions sparing of energy, all my motion subservient to the central figure of my grief.

She says, "Please don't waste your energy trying to remember who I am. I don't think we have ever met. But I came anyway. I am here only as a mother."

In a moment of recognition the strange woman and I leave the house, the city, the country. We soar through space. We are mothers praying together at the Tomb of the Mother Rachel. Where she wept for her children in exile,[13] we have a foothold, a corner of earth that is in sympathy with our mission.

She accompanies me briefly on the journey, her hand in mine. Her tears mix indelibly with mine and taste indistinguishable from my own. Because we are strangers, the woman and I are free to know each other behind ourselves, beyond the features of ordinary familiarity. Because we are strangers, we are free to find the common thread that weaves in us: our motherhood, our common tradition.

Together we enter the exile from the familiar that has been imposed by death. "*Lech lecha.*"[14] Go you unto yourself, Abraham is told at the dawn of our collective birth. He begins an epic exile from the familiar that courses through us still. It is an epic act because what our Fathers did "is a sign for their children."[15] His exile from the familiar, this way of being rootless in the world in order to stay rooted to God, this becomes emblematic in our character.

"*Lech lecha*" still speaks in us. Leave your land, your birthplace, says the voice. Leave the house of your father. Leave utterly these familiar places where you have grown familiar with yourself in relation to others. Enter the stream of your inner existence until you are alone. Go into the crux of yourself. Free yourself to discover the ultimate point of contact with the *Ribbono shel Olam.*

This is the exile we journey back to. This is the exile that charts a path on my journey.

On the last night of the *shivah*, exhausted from the inner streaming and the strength of the human stream, my husband and I retire. Out of the corner of my eye, as we turn on the staircase I see a couple enter the house.

This story belongs to the children who remain in the room. At first they are impatient to get the visit over with. The hour is late. They want to find snacks and go to bed. But the couple stays, saying nothing.

An aunt, concerned for the children's rest, asks the couple if they know us. "No," they reply, and sink into silence. After several moments the aunt asks them what brings them here.

I can see them now through the children's description, the words pouring from them, the pouring out of their gestures into their words of loss.

They describe the kindness of Yosef. As they talk, they add more lines to the sketch we had only dimly sensed of our son. From the words of strangers, we learn of the extent of his devotion to people. We experience a sudden shift. A loss-gain-loss to know the son we knew, the one we never knew, until now we know him through the eyes of the unknown, only to lose him once again.

He knew worlds that were unknown to us. While he mastered our lessons on love and caring, he surpassed us in the cultivation of pure kindness. Now, in order to recall the taste of the grapes, we have to look to the wine.

He was not a little boy after all. We did not define for him the limits of the world, the boundaries of home. He was at home in the world. In a way, he became for us during the *shivah* an Unknown.

How little do we know of those known to us. In our overdrawn image of the familiar, we rob ourselves daily of the mysterious unknown within each person who is known to us.

The next morning after *shacharit*, *shivah* is over.

We stay gathered in the room as the children tell us about the last visitor. One of them says: Just think how many others had stories to tell about Yosef that we did not get to hear.

To console them, an uncle tells them a story, a transcendent tale of unknown visitors that anyone can own.

The Talmud[16] tells of an old man who dies leaving no survivors who could gather to comfort him. Now you might wonder, intones the uncle, if the man was dead why would he need anyone to comfort him? What comfort does a dead man need? His soul has already left his body and returned to God.

But just as we mourn a person's death because he will be separated from us, so does the man's soul mourn for his body. For, while the *neshamah* returns gladly to God, the body dies. The soul mourns for the body who was its friend, its faithful servant in performing the mitzvot.

And so, when the old man died and there was no one who knew him to mourn for him and comfort him, Rabbi Yehudah gathered a group of people to sit in the dead man's house every day for seven days. After the seventh day the dead man appeared to Rabbi Yehudah in a dream: "You may rest easy," he said, "because now I can rest."

❧

At the best of times I am impatient with small talk. Someone who comes to visit us comments on our lovely old fireplace.

A moment fails between us. A moment dies between us. How can we meet in this moment if you hide behind the fireplace? Maybe you imagine that the fireplace will offer me a distraction. It doesn't.

I ask you what you really want to say to me. You cry and say: I do not know.

That is satisfying. Tears. Silence. A fitting memorial. A fitting expression of the overwhelming feelings. What a profound way to reach out to us.

I imagine your tears make a bridge. A silvery delicate bridge. A filigree bridge. An intricate structure between us. When I can speak again, I will know the way to your house. You came and went from our sad house. You leave a trail of tears. You enter our pain. You do not abandon us.

Between us stretches a bridge of tears. It is so strong no one can break it.

The Visitor

It is a blustery day, fall is turning. Winter is on its heels. The gentle qualities in the winds, in the leaves that blanket the bare branches, and in the soft, wavering grasses are gone.

What sustains me when the clouds are cumulus, overbearing, inescapable?

What of a day when the view is hazy, the way unclear? What of days and weeks when I am thrown back onto the minuteness of my perspective? And in the minuteness I am imprisoned in pain, in desolation and confusion.

I lift my face to the wind. Against the stormy backdrop, a flock of birds sails past. I stand and watch until they are out of sight. And then, long after they are gone, afterimages remain of soft and mysterious formations. I am flooded now with streams of images, offerings, rituals of love and sharing that have come to me since Yosef died.

I see the family, my husband and children, as we move together through the scenes of loss and ritualized mourning. Synchronized as the flock of birds, we follow the silent command of the heart to act as one. As the dancers twist and weave around each other, each gesture is inclined toward the inner circle, each movement seems to have in it the pattern of the whole dance.

With this dance we are strengthened. We are reminded that together we are more than we are alone. Our dance graces and expands us.

Now we are spent. Resting near each other, we each await a visitor, the energy that must come from outside ourselves.

You enter the room. I have to raise my chin and lift my eyes and look up through the vast space that separates you, standing upright in your fresh street clothes, and me, huddled down in my worn clothing in the lowest spot in the room, all bends and rounded angles turning inward, inward.

When you see me, you run swiftly to me. I feel your arms gather me up. I hear the sound of your voice in my ear before I can sort out meanings. In between the rustle, rustle that we create coming together, I can hear the sound of your heart. It is near and insistent. I focus intently on it until all other sounds are sent back into the distance like the sound that remains after the waves have hit the shore and receded.

As I am held, I begin to sense myself in ways I have not done since the first awful moment. I sense my spatial dimensions, where I begin and leave off. Against your cheek I know the contours of my face. In your hand, I feel the limits of my hand. In your arms, I feel confirmed, confident of something I was unsure of, until now.

It is the perception of my own wholeness you deliver back to me in your embrace. I have tumbled through the accident, the shattering whirring terrible impact. I have been thrown and broken a hundred times over. I understand that it is I who lay on the side of the road abandoned, whimpering, lost even to my own sense of myself. In your arms I begin to heal.

Now words. The words you will say will be so important, so vital to me that the entire process of the giving and receiving plays itself out in slowed down motion. The words are born in your will, they will be given form in your brain and sent along a message trail to your throat. As they emerge from your throat I order my will to receive, to prepare the ear to catch the sound waves, the brain to sort out the perception into meaning. Here, I have unwrapped the gift; it is ready for me now.

"All the way over here, ever since I heard Yosef was killed" (no, you don't flinch from these words or from me) "I have been thinking. You are locked in a prison. We must find a way to let you out. Then the strength will flow from you to Hillel and your children, from you, from you. You'll see. You will be the medium... But first there must be a key..."

I hear my voice responding. It is rusty and halting, as if it were years and not days since I had last spoken. But I am broken. You are whole. You are strong. You have strength. I am not like you.

Your answer is to laugh and smile and cry.

Together, the tears begin to flow and wash away the unshed tears in the dry soul, and in the flowing, the soul begins to give up the restraint of its deep, dry recesses.

Already I am past my words, already I am busy with your vision of me. Already I can see that I am in prison, I begin to imagine the possibility of an opening, a door, a key.

What is this place we enter soul-to-soul?
Each day you come and go.
Inside I bid you to enter.
Past the first room
Where all the mourners sit,
Past the second room
Where all the comforters are gathered
Past the next room where I am set in stone
Shocked into still life form of petrified rock
Unable to see myself move
Past the next room
That is so crowded with self pity
That sorrow overflows the space.
Utter uncertainty for the future,
Past the room where anger rears its head,
And leaves me limp with rejection.
Now into a quiet room.
It is an empty room.
You permit me alone to furnish it.
I furnish it with my dreams.
I fill it with my images.
In it there are no interpretations

No theories of consolation.
There is only the reality of my mind
And this moment.
There is only one sound in the room.
It is the sound of you listening.
Here I seek my memories,
Here I salvage my sense of self.
Here I recreate the son.
Here I recreate the mother.
Here I feel you holding me holding him
Holding one another indistinguishable
Until it is once again clear who we are.

One day, later on in time, it will be this room, this scene that will enable the woman to arise and go.

One day on in time she will know that she is still a *zivug* in the choreography of the *Ribbono shel Olam*. One day she will once again seek to create a dance that is worthy of her partner, her spiritual shadow, the sister image she has not yet grown into but senses once again. And when she does, it will be this room this place these reflections soul-to-soul that enable her to rise and go. "As water reflects the face of a person, so the heart of a person reflects the other..."[17]

As a psychotherapist and as a friend, I have made many prison calls. I have entered into the darkness, into the perceptual prison of others. Only when the prisoners could see me beside them, sharing their pain, could they begin to take in that I had the freedom to come and go. It is this awareness that spells

the beginnings of release. Together, then, we could begin to ex-
amine options, escape routes, keys, openings we had not con-
sidered before. As the Talmud says, "A man cannot release himself from prison."[18]

The release must start with another, another pair of eyes
which takes in the entire scene. The prisoner's release is contin-
gent on his awareness that he is in prison. The other one shows
the way, the other one defines the dimensions of the prison, the
distinction between the prisoner's position and the free one.

Now it is I, I who am wrapped up in the roundness of grief,
round rock-round, bound around with no opening no mouth to
grieve aloud with. Like the roundness of the egg which is the traditional mourning food, I lack a *pitchon peh*, an open mouth. No
matter how many prison calls I have made, no matter how faithful a visitor I have been, I cannot use those experiences for my
own release. Alone, the one who is locked up lacks the means to
express the dimensions of her own imprisonment.

There have been others, there have been hands and hearts
that have taught me where I am. And no matter how deep the
dungeon, no matter how devoid of light, there has been the
voice of the true companion saying: I am behind you, beside
you, with you. I do not flinch in the dark. I do not withhold myself from you in your pain.

This is a way that requires courage and risk-taking. And
flexibility in one's vision to take in the shifts that have taken
place, the sudden exchange of myself from guide to prisoner.
Many refuse to take this trip with me. Some insist that I display
strength and therapeutic powers even now in the rawness of

tragedy. Some are unwilling to revise their image of me. They stay away and stay away, sometime calling to say "how are you?" carefully defending against any genuine acknowledgment of my loss. Unwilling to revise their notion of me as Strong and Wise, and Independent, they refuse to enter the prison in which I experience loss, pain, weakness, fear, and aloneness.

They make a myth of me: She doesn't want visitors. She prefers to be alone. She will do this best by herself. She is so strong there isn't anything that I can think of that I have that she needs.

I cry out at you, Myth Makers. You make a myth of me. He is dead and you deaden me, confining me to the narrow lines you choose for me. You send me to another prison when I need you to confirm that I am alive. I still reel from the hurt in your silence. The pain of your abandonment.

I am angry that you protect yourself when it is I who needs protection. I am angry at spending my diminished energy crying over my tears, tears for you.

It is three months since my son died. It is light-years in distances spanned, ground covered. What will we be to each other when we meet again? We will meet like former classmates who have not seen each other in so many years that the questions they ask each other, the frame for any inquiry, will be ludicrous.

The estrangement is the pain of living deadness.

❧❧

Yosef's death makes me feel as if I am branded. On my forehead is written the sign, Bereaved Mother. I feel like an uncomely character creeping out of the woods. I feel stigmatized. Nobody is sure what to say.

Better than words are loving looks, your heart shining in your eyes like lights that signal each other in the night. Or outstretched arms, the brief moment of a hand on the shoulder, the melon left at the door when you went shopping and wondered how to bring some sweetness to our house.

I begin to think about every person who had been touched by grief, handicap, illness. I imagine us together in need of comfort. In need of Hashem's mercy. In my loneliness I sense the vast circle of pain.

We must not hide or be hidden no matter how uncomfortable we make others. We must reach out to each other and give to each other. Two are better than one. We must share strengths because in the checkerboard of our weaknesses and strengths we support each other.

We must not hide or be hidden. We must teach the rest of the world not to look away. No matter how sad we look.

No one is sure what to say. We can accept the silence; not the abandonment.

How Are You?

My research on childhood illness reveals that we are not equipped to assess how well a person with an illness is doing. We are plagued with a pathogenic bias. We aren't used to responding realistically. We aren't in the habit of saying: Considering the magnitude of the illness, the impact of the challenges, this person or family copes well. Instead we hold onto our usual standards. Then in our assessments we over-focus on variations from normal, forgetting that illness is itself a variation.

Now loss. Now grief. I am frequently asked, How Are You?

It is only a few weeks since my son died. I am practically non-functioning. I can't work, read, shop, cook, converse, concentrate, or stand up for long. I can't remember things. I lose things. I cry until I am thirsty. I can't decide things.

Practically pathological by normal standards.

But, considering where I've been it is just right.

So How Are You, REALLY?

I am grieving. I am intense. Alone. Suffering. I am working

hard to stand still, to not fall. I am grieving.

But how ARE you?

And the Song of the Innocent continues. It persists, and it drowns out other realities — illness, death, aging, handicap. It denies deviation from the norm. So strong is the myth of normality, so persistent the self-persuasion that the weak, old, sick, dying, and bereaved are rendered invisible.

The voice of the innocent is intentional and embedded in the simple words "how are you?" Beneath the banality is a cruel demand. Deliver an answer. It contains Three and only Three words and each word contains One and only One syllable. Reinforce my reality. Comfort me. I demand that you remain consistent with my needs. Be what I wish you to be. Be that which will cause me no pain, no confusion, no need to reevaluate my mind. Be fine. Let me admit not your impediment.

With words we cocreate each other — or we annihilate each other, twice over. For the lonely, handicapped, bereaved, ill, old, and dying have lost their language to start with. They find themselves on a silent journey, wordless in the match between their experience and the familiar. They are lost in the terror of a strange landscape. Not only do we fail to empower them, to confirm them, to name them, to name in relative configuration, to place them on a vital continuum of the living, but we silence them. Wordless, shocked and hurt, we confine them to three syllables. We insist they mouth our words and abandon further their task of creating themselves.

Already exiled from their former sense of self, we exile them from our connectivity.

⸭

Teshuvah is about becoming different.

The words of Rav Shlomo Freifeld, z"l, forge a direct pathway to my heart. Was he speaking just for me? Did he know that I could not face Rosh HaShanah with twice empty arms? No son. No reviving sense of change. No teshuvah to light up my prayers.

No teshuvah? My world has been turned upside down and shaken. I am still drifting down like snowflakes in a miniature globe.

No teshuvah? I have strained to seek Hashem from the depths of my pain. I seek Him from a new place. An awful place. But I seek Him.

I see how I am different.

I seek Him from any place I find myself. If I can seek Him from any place, any mood, any state of being, I have just begun to realize the vastness of worship. How I can be marooned on a desert island, or marooned from myself and still seek Him.

Let this be my offering.

Turning Corners

*I*t is the eve of Rosh HaShanah. Where has the time gone? How did the month of Av become Elul, and how is Elul about to turn a corner and become Tishrei? Pain precludes the usual perception of the passing of time. I am an immigrant in the land of the living. I wander about, missing old landmarks.

What became of *Teshuvah*, Repentance, Return? The season for my usual preoccupation with Return has almost passed. The season filled with straining after deeper connections to oneself, to the world, and to God, the season in which I can sense the availability of God's help in my relationship to Him, is swiftly passing.

I am too tired, too weak, to engage myself in the effort in the usual way. I wonder how it will seem to stand there on the Days of Awe and show Him, palms upward, my empty hands.

I wonder if there is still a link that I can retrieve. I don't know how I will get through the Holy Days this year at all. If I could hold on to something, if I could somehow plug myself into the *teshuvah* current...

As I am about to light the Sabbath candles this thought flickers in me: "*Teshuvah* is not about becoming better; it is about becoming different."[19] If change is the prerequisite to *teshuvah*, I am highly qualified. I will never be the same. I am working to hold on in the eye of the storm. As long as I can sense the sustained presence of the *Ribbono shel Olam* throughout the storm, this will be my *teshuvah* offering.

Despite the consolation I offer myself, Rosh HaShanah is a time of desolation, pain, and complete exhaustion. The Holy Day schedule demands that I give up my timeless flowing and give over to the structure of the day. I am not equipped to confront time. My grieving keeps me in a protective cloud of timelessness.

Even when I pray in the familiar prayer book for the Days of Awe, I lose my way again and again. Then for long moments I seem to merge with the prayer for Hope, *Tikvah tovah l'dorshecha* — Good hope to those who seek it.[20]

Afterward I am even more drained and pulled down, even more depleted. I agree to take my older daughters to the Rebbe's traditional *teshuvah* talk before Yom Kippur. He explores the potency of the process of *teshuvah*, the ultimate rejuvenative potential that can carry us "up until God."[21] In *teshuvah*, he explains, the individual can become a reflection of God. The process of purification results in a reflection of God that is visible in the person.

Greeting us at the door, my husband comments that I look

different. As he listens, I try out this idea: If the power of *teshuvah* is transforming to the extent that we become different entities, it will be THIS potential that will enable me to transcend the tragedy. It is not my former self, but my transformed one who can begin to transcend.

With these words I feel freer than I have felt since the first moment of the tragedy. I feel the tentative beginnings of looking forward. I begin to see myself emerge from the amorphous, timeless cloud. Looking forward is healing; it implies the future. The past and present shape themselves around this construct.

The mother of Yosef, the one who bore him, and nursed him, and worried for him, and took delight in him was not constructed to absorb and accept the tragedy. She is constitutionally incapable. She IS mother to the boy. This defines her. She cannot be released. To accept his death is simply not possible for her.

It is too radical, too dissonant, too counter a force to her existence. It reminds me of the biblical maxim that no angel is sent to the world with two missions.[22] The mind and heart of the mother are inclined toward her child. Her mission and her identity are one force.

I am changed. I am not the same person. In my lifetime I have watched *ba'alei teshuvah*. The potential that allows a person to contemplate her relative position to God, the potential that enables a person to shift awareness to the extent that she places the *Ribbono shel Olam* at the very center of her perception of the world, this potential is human, it lives in me. This potential will enable me to release myself from the prison of the perceptual world of the "first mother."

As I see that Yosef's existence is in a different place, I sense that my constellation is shifting. In a vast and dark sky, I seek the strange pattern of lights that forms my new constellation. I ask the *Ribbono shel Olam* to be my guide.

꙳

On the ship which took my mother's family from Turkey to America in the early 1920s, a severe storm arose. The captain feared for the safety of the passengers. In the midst of this storm, my grandfather, a"h, gathered his children on deck. He asked them to keep Shabbat for the rest of their lives.

When he heard each of them promise, he was satisfied. Perhaps God was, too. The storm abated.

When they reached America, his children remained true to their word. The lure to wealth, materialism, and Sabbath desecration did not overtake them as it did so many immigrants to America. It was their freedom he was securing.

Shabbat is a miniature of the World to Come, he reasoned. If you keep Shabbat, one-seventh of you is free from the material demands of the world. From one-seventh, you may divine the rest.

Shabbat will be your teacher. Wherever you find yourself, Shabbat will free your spirit and lift it from the traps of this world. Shabbat will guide your soul back to God.

One day, in the most intense moments of mourning, the spirit of Shabbat visits me.

Holy Days

The cycle of Holy Days continues.

There is Sukkot, there is Simchat Torah. I am not ready for these times. I am so full of sorrow that *simchah*, joy, pushes at me rudely demanding its turn. I am powerless against its tune and its insistent rhythm.

I am a newly hatched fish carried along by the current. Am I swimming? I suppose so, but it seems to bear little resemblance to the active exercise that I can remember that involved volition, concentration, effort, and timing.

Nor does this passive movement of the newly wrought form bear any resemblance to more primitive half memories of movement within movement, suspended echoes, the promise of time that is still deeply held within the vault of the unborn.

I am not ready. I am thin of skin, vulnerable. I long to drop back into the sea, de-evolving back into time to a simpler form. I seek my self before I am sufficiently differentiated to warrant such fragmentization.

I dream of the descent

shedding layers of false cover
the landing in the soft mud
the single-eyed view
up through the dappled miles
the expanse of light and space
merged in gentle refraction
There, I am held in the arms of timeless motion
free to dream on of an open future.

I long for a moment in time that feels lost. I long for the place in between me and God. I reach deeper and deeper into myself, past word to memory, past memory to image, past the image to the dream, past the layers of dream to the heart of the dream.

I sift through terror for the Light. Somewhere within me is the realm of being in which my people and history live. It comes before me, it streams through me. It will live after me. It unites all creation. It enters my sleep with vision of another time, other places. Its voice calls to me in dreams, in poetic images I make my own. Its vowels play in my consciousness. Its syllables shape my thoughts. I awaken to ancient dreams. There is a path underlying the cosmos. Its blueprint is the Torah.[23] I am willing to follow its traces. I am willing to suspend judgment. I am willing to loosen my rootedness in the world to seek it. When I expose myself to my poverty, to the sheer longing for the Light, it responds. It reveals itself. It permits me reentry into the Light that is held within the vessels of Tradition. Into the space between person and God.

With its gift I begin to awaken from the soft cloud of my misery. The reentry into time is a healing. It connects my dream and vision to the collective voice of my people that lives in me, to the Torah, to the cycle of Sabbath, to the New Moon and the Holy Days. To the Points of Light in the dark landscape.

It is the week of the Torah reading of Genesis. Three themes dance and weave around me:

The cycle is never finished without a new beginning.

Creating is constant and constant in me.

Genesis is Yosef's portion, the one read the week he was born, the one he read for us at his bar mitzvah.

The dark waters whirling around me feel less strange at this moment.

The current that carries me is flowing in Torah time, its ancient rhythm familiar to me.

It beats the rhythm of creation that links to my people, to Eternity, to my son.

The current not only pushes and pulls me, it Becomes me.

Sabbath Eve.

The family members from out of town have left. The friends who came from near and far have gone home. The house is empty of its overflow of take-home foods. It is time to look at the raw ingredients and imagine again how to cook.

The exertion of the trip to the store is beyond my level of energy. Gravity pulls at me. It is an effort of will to hold up my head. It costs me pain in strained muscles to stand upright. The head wants to curl forward. The neck wants no claim of independence. I make up the grocery list. I give it to the children. When they return with the bags and the tumult, I wonder how to make a start at this task. I wonder what is the task.

Here are the vegetables, the meat, the chicken, the fish. What makes it so difficult to send my hands through the motions? What had I been bringing to the task that is missing now?

There is no son to cook for. Of all the family members and guests I have cooked for, Yosef was my intended audience. For sixteen years I cooked for the glint of joy in his eyes. Appreciation flowed easily from him. He acknowledged my effort.

There is so much love in food, and Yosef and I spoke its language well.

Here is my labor of love, well seasoned and carefully prepared. I have taken the stuff of life and transformed it for you into something you can use. Eat, be strong and grow in Torah...

This, Mom, is the best food, love, strength, transformation, message anyone ever gave me...

But Shabbat is coming and must be honored. We all must eat. I cannot buy prepared foods; these will not help me now. I make a start. I begin to entice my reluctant hands into the task. I find it is Shabbat I am speaking to. I sing to myself. *Heilige Shabbos, taiyere Shabbos*. Holy Sabbath, Dear Sabbath. I cannot prepare for my son. Let me prepare for your spirit.

I begin. The kitchen is bright, the sunlight senses a happening and wants to join us. It dances around the room, and reflects my song in the rhythm of its movements. Fingers start to fly, to obey and will. The food is being transformed in color and texture and smell. The sweet and spicy steam fills the air and covers the inside of the windows. The contents of pots are bubbling, the inside of the oven emits the intrigue of snapping and popping sounds. All forms of matter that are within the sphere of my influence are inclined now to the task. I sense in them the joy of purpose, the fulfillment of service.

As I speak with words of the heart to the spirit of Sabbath I am calmer, more peaceful and in harmony than I have been for many weeks.

This world is the corridor to the World to Come. Whoever prepares on the eve of Sabbath will enjoy the fruits of his labors on Shabbat.[24] Although it is a preparation, a means and not an end, it is the WAY, the vehicle to the experience of eternity in the next world, to Sabbath in this world. The eve of Sabbath is our mode of being in the world.

Throughout the time of intense grieving, there is a terrible struggle. To hold on, to not give way to the overwhelming emptiness in the house since my son has gone, the overwhelming pain at his empty place at the Sabbath table.

The world we are familiar with is changed for me. With the death of my son came an immeasurable shift in perception. I cannot feel the pleasure and predictable sense of comfort I once knew here.

Sabbath eve sustains me. In its enactment I find myself. The promise in the message of Sabbath eve I read and reread like a letter from a beloved: Take the stuff of life. Now begin. Join in.

Transform it. I will help you. I will make the sunlight join. I will send the energy flowing in. It will carry you forever.

I am a stranger here. I have lost my familiar foothold. I have experienced death in a finite world. My sense of future, of projection, feels dead. But Sabbath eve sings in me. Promise, it says. Process, it says. Be fully in the moment in the present, it says. Immerse yourself in the preparation for its own sake. I am not a finite quantity but a value. Become intertwined in my quality. Remember: I love and I hold you dear.

I forget who is singing to whom.

❧❧

The inscape is an awesome place. It is a deep terrain full of steep turns and surprises. It is not a place we want to dwell in. It is too stark. Too lonely.

But, I had to go there. The death seemed to propel me to deep silent canyons of the spirit. I discover a language for my loss. I scream.

But then the scream is finished. I breathe deep. I seem to find a clearing in my lungs that had been crowded. What will I find there?

I find laughter. If my scream is the scream of knowing too much, of the burden of death; then the laughter is the laughter of a child. That is what I am. A child. A sad, sweet daughter of Hashem. I laugh my way closer to You. I say to You: I do not know too much. I know You are my Father. Take care of me.

The Inscape

Four months...I seem to carry myself above myself. I offer myself the softest shoulder to rest against, against which sounds are muffled and the impact of the journey absorbed. I step carefully over the pieces of things that are too sharp.

One day I awaken with my teeth on edge. Everything seems set at too sharp an angle. The day's activities refuse to flow. They seem to pile up like a bunch of unwieldy objects on a wagon trying to make its way uphill. The skill of the driver and the strain of the horse can pull the wagon over the rough climb, but no force can make the odd cargo balance itself for the pull.

Late in the afternoon I go to visit a friend. She is away, but her cat sits by her front door. When I bend to stroke his familiar gray coat, he suddenly bites me. The pain gallops along the nerve trail and I yell out loud. Then I begin to cry out loud. The cat is startled and retreats from me, but it is I who go in defeat.

For a few days I am sick. The flu. A fever keeps me in bed. There I am free once more to float over myself. I land on nothing softer than clouds. I see my face smiling at my son's face smiling at me through a radiant light. I will be well for Shabbat, I tell myself, and I am.

The day is clear and cold. I walk to shul. Next to me a young woman is praying and crying. I look at her. I let her see me seeing her. She says, "I was raised in an observant home and went away. Now I know how my bitterness at my parents propelled me away. Now I choose to be here but I don't know if I really belong."

"Sister, I hear your song, it enters my being and teaches itself to my soul. It is a noble song, a song of pure pain, this aching after belonging, this yearning for the root that is surely hidden under the snow. Is your journey so different from any of ours?"

"Isn't it?"

"What is the journey but TOWARD Him? Even the turning Away is defined by the turning Toward."

We look long into each other's eyes, melting away the great ice walls, and when she briefly takes my hand it is warm and restful in mine.

We each turn to pray, to settle into the inner journey. Now we spin away away, in through the inmiles, passing the ingates, entering the deep inscape, once more Alone.

Now winding, spiraling upward, flying on the wings of an upturned palm, an upturned cheek, a light eye, a lifted chin, we enter on the strength of pure will, this inclining, this bending Toward.

I bend into the silent devotion, the *Amidah*, a reed pliant and beautiful in its fluid grace. I meet the letters that spell the words that form the vessels that shape my will. I pour myself into these.

Suddenly my hand lands heavily on my shoulder holding me still. I am shocked into stillness. I listen. What I hear is my own voice screaming into the vast reaches, into the miles deeper into the inscape than I have ever dared go. The scream is pure sound, it is a stick against sand, it is a hand against velvet, a moment against Time. It is full and fine and billowy and strong. I am startled listening to myself.

I begin to laugh. It is a soundless laugh that carries me deeper inward and over a current of blue skies, through cities of cloud miles, beyond any reaches I have traveled toward You. I lift my face.

> *I will not leave You.*
> *I will not run away in terror*
> *At my own voice.*
> *I am true.*
> *A child,*
> *My face is set*
> *In relief against You,*
> *In my scream I seek You*
> *In my call I search for You*
> *In my powerlessness*
> *I bend myself toward You.*
> *I serve You with my emptiness.*
> *I honor You in my suffering.*

To serve You I give away a child,
I become a child again
And go out lonely
Into the wild places
An orphan defining herself
By her emptiness,
Knowing herself by what she lacks.
Her entire being
Reduced,
Distilled,
Refined into the one crux point
Longing for the root
And thirsting
Thirsting after relatedness.
I am here my true Father
I create my trueness of You in my
Trueness of child.
I seek You and find myself.
I sense You wherever I seek You.
I lift my face.
This too is an offering.

❧

In my husband's neighborhood when he was small, there was a boy who lived disconnected from reality. We don't know the nature of his dysfunction. My husband was only five when he remembers this story.

He was walking on the street with his parents when they saw the boy. The boy spoke about his dead brother as if he were alive. Why do you speak that way, said the small boy who would be my husband. Everyone knows that's not the truth.

Hush said the boy's parents. Hush.

How can death be denied? If we choose denial over acceptance, we become crazy, disconnected from reality. Time, a flowing changing river stops. Water that stands becomes stagnant. It takes more and more energy to pretend. To not grow. To stunt ourselves. To remain like statues in the original position.

Early on, we decide we would not say Hush. We would let the river flow. We would let go. Yosef himself helps us in this choice. He is simply too alive, too vibrant and funny and smart and sweet to freeze into a still life. He is still moving around and making things happen. He still makes us laugh and cry. He is still teaching us how to live.

The last time I see him is the day after Tishah B'Av. He is reluctant to shave off his beard that grew over the three weeks. Indeed, in his beard he looks much older and can fool people into thinking he is not just sixteen.

He says he is getting down to the shave. He comes in. I see

only the unshaved part. Well? I ask. He turns and shows me the neatly shaved part. His face is evenly divided between boy and man. We laugh at his wit, his commentary on the half-way state of sixteen, the double take of a sixteen-year-old boy.

The next day he dies. Only partway to adult.

I have to remember the laughter. It was real. It happened. His antics. I have to let the laughter have way. Yosef made us laugh.

Half tears, half laughter, the demarcation line is life. Yosef still teaches us how to live.

Time and Reality

It is four months since Yosef died. I go with a friend to the ocean, to a hotel famous for its watery therapies. The ocean in December. It is vast and manifest in full force without the softening effects of sun, warming breezes, and people. The ocean in December is time playing itself out against eternity.

In massage therapy I learn how I have developed the habit of storing my tension in my neck. When the therapist's hands discover the knots of tension, I have an urge to hide, to cry. I surprise myself by saying: I see that you found where I keep it.

I feel even more defenseless as she works to ease the tension out of my muscles. What purpose was this to me that I was frightened, too defeated to let it go?

I am pampered, steamed, whirlpooled, relaxed, and worried. During all these treatments I feel exposed, suspended, buoyant, and vulnerable. Even my secret cache of tension has been discovered. The daily vistas of the vast, turbulent ocean do little to minimize my sense of defenselessness.

What have I hidden, what secret message have I written, encapsulated, and entrusted to the inner recesses of my neck?

My sense of being found out hurts and amuses me...it renders my acts of concealment useless, my acts of denial futile. When we speak of denial of death, what is it we mean? I fall asleep wondering what face of denial has hidden itself in my anatomy.

I dream I am returning to my home after the brief vacation. I go to see my husband, but he is away from his office. I wait for him. When he arrives he is agitated and tired. He tells me that our son wasn't in school where he was supposed to be.

I am thrown into chaotic confusion. At first, I cannot speak at all.

When I do speak I see myself in front of a mirror addressing myself: But isn't Yosef dead? Didn't he die four months ago? Didn't I just go on a brief trip in order to rest, the first night spent away from home since he died? But what Hillel is saying is so convincing that I cannot decide.

I am thrown into a welter of confusion. Time signals clash; they leave me suspended in a timeless zone. Stripped of my usual set of landmarks, I am floating on an utterly strange sea.

I try to defend against this confusion. I try to deny it. Somewhere deep in my neck I hide my doubt. Only now, in the dream, do I acknowledge that the terrible confusion is a part of my experience.

We depend on time. We cling to this thing we know, that there was a past, that there is a present, that there will be a future. Time is the landmark in an otherwise vast and amorphous territory. It helps us to a feeling of familiarity and control. In death, there is a dramatic disruption, an utter chaos that time used to direct.

Death makes us question the taken-for-granted sequence. Death blows the facade off the familiar structure, and we are left to confront living stripped of its usual frame. Death confuses me, it confuses me. It keeps me from my former sense of reality. If I stick to my simple former notion of past, present, and future I cannot fit in that I had a son, that he lived, that he helped define us all. That he lived and co-created our identity and ceased to be confuses me.

Because he just died I focus on him, his voice, his face, my experience of our life together. Then this experience becomes so vivid, so real, that I am jolted awake against the fact that it must be memory, since he is already dead.

If he is dead, then maybe so am I. I become confused: the future excludes him and my long-held sense of self.

I know there is no easy equation to resolve the confusion. I take the confusion that would have annihilated me four months ago and stick it in the vault, deep in my neck. I pay for it in strained muscles, but I am not ready to own it outright.

Behind the dramatic veils of the dream, in the guise of my husband and I as two people, I can see the clashing faces of reality. While the dream resolves nothing, it does serve to shrink the distance between my encapsulated fear and my conscious awareness of it. I confront my fear of chaotic confusion. I am getting used to its dimensions. I retreat into irony.

Take your Choice, I say to myself. Will you prefer Denial of Uncertainty or Uncertainty?

Before I go home I accept from the staff a prescription for the relaxation of strained neck muscles. I thank them for having served me.

Death is tough enough and then it finds allies. Inside us, there are injuries, weaknesses, whole areas that we don't like, old places of shame. The Gray Lady is an old persona that hangs around my murky dark corners. When Yosef dies, she takes up the old refrain: *If something bad happened, someone is to blame.*

On top of the weight of loss comes the weight of blame and guilt.

It is too much.

It is too heavy.

It is not what Hashem wants.

He wants us to accept the unknown. To live with it. To be changed by it. He wants us to heal. He wants to touch us in mystery and love. He does not want us to be crushed.

Old critical voices merge with the pain. They need to be routed out. Finally.

To survive the death I need all the strength I can find. I have to be sure I am not making it worse.

During the shivah my friend notices that one of my young daughters is not eating. For a small moment I take her away from the crowd of visitors, into the safe passage of a quiet room, onto my lap. I stroke her pale face. I want her to tell me.

I say that sometimes people are pale from sadness. Sometimes from not eating.

She tells me. She does not know why she is not eating. I

know because I know her. I know myself. I know how we are
constructed. In the face of the awful unknown, we look for ex-
planations, even painful, self-inflicting, puny ones. We seem to
hate the vacuum. We fill it, with bad ideas.

I say to her: Hashem took Yosef, not you.

You must live.

She eats.

The Gray Lady and Me

Yosef is dead. He's dead. The call said he is dead. That he died in a car accident. I will never see my son again, never touch him, never watch him grow. That is what dead is.

My family is torn. My husband is sonless, my girls have no brother.

I am one-sixth dead, one part of me is disconnected from the rest. It will die off. Choked off from its source, this mother of Yosef must die too.

I beseech myself: Talk to me, talk to me. Create an order, a structure in chaos. Tell me that everything is not dead. That yet there lives process that does not add up and reduce irrevocably down to death.

Start with what you know. That God lives is a certainty. There is the irony that nothing is so certain as God once you face death. You're not even sure you have patience for anything less than Eternity.

Talk keep talking, make sounds that make words that create sense. Keep talking gently murmuring easy, sweetly, softly...don't stop. I am afraid.

I am too tired to keep on. I cannot keep up the pace. What of a little silence? Is it so threatening?

Lady in Gray appears with big fists punching the air: You LOST him. YOU lost HIM. You LOST him. YOU worthless excuse for a mother.

She finds me so undefended. In the vicious circle of her words I am rolled, pushed, pulled and sent downhill at forty miles an hour head over heel, over and over myself every turn an endless bruise.

She begins to push round words through the opening of my mouth: Why did he drive the car? Why did you let him go? Why didn't you keep an eye on him, an eye of an eagle-eyed hawk or at the very least a hawk-eyed mother. You are nothing, adding to Zero Mother: otherwise (notice the down curve now)

how do you go

and lose him

your only

your precious son.

The mountain of your accusation blocks the sun paths and one day seems like a moon's worth of turnings. My own face turns heel on me and I gasp and gasp for the sheer light of day.

Rain on me like rain, the blessings of peace, the message of truth, the perception of light. Shine on me like sun, the rays of light, the sense of truth...I remember the sunbaths in the baby carriage my mother gave me so religiously...I feel the scratch of the soft blanket the yarn tied fringes under my chin. I feel the sunlight through my closed eyelids.

You know in your strange and powerful wordless wonder that you don't open your eyes against the blinding brightness. You have to own this by yourself since no one protects you from it, but if there is no one to share this with, you are also spared anyone pumping into you the logic that since you can't open your eyes there is no proof of the existence of light. I know before I am verbal that Something precedes essence.

Later a pinpoint follows me into darkness, rays poking into the prison wheel me down to the original spoke of my existence, turning me. Yes, I will too turn around the rock, bound around, opening at lips with no mouth to even grieve with; create an opening the slice of a needle's eye passing ageless time-ripened praise.

I wrap up for me the prespective of God who is hidden around and around me like a grateful beggar a shawl with familiar feeling fringes. Through my dark lids I perceive Him.

I use this shining light to travel by. I leave behind my country/my orientation, my birthplace/my identity, my father's house/my claim to innocence. I go me unto me. I leave guilt off the stove away from the flame, the coals turning dull and lifeless. Black rages I turn on its side to convert its energy. Responsibility I give away with the ownership of my son.

I begin to rest —

— Oh you do, do you? Can a mother ever rest? What of the rest? What will become of you, you who lost him, lost him, lost him.

Look, Gray Lady, lost is just another word...I can tell you something about this word. Once me and my five-year-old cousin were walking home alone from kindergarten he lost the five dollar tablecloth that the five dollar bill from his mother had turned into at the school office by the hand of the lady named the secretary who didn't smile and wore wrinkled eyes...I remember a lady who was fat only in the front who had so much extra she smiled and didn't walk around much and one day she was very bad, having lost her baby. Bad boys and ladies lose things or fives or tablecloths or the babies hidden under the corners of the dresses she wore.

One day I call to her,

— Gray Lady, come here, I want to see you better

— Who wants me?

— Why just a little girl who doesn't even know what L-M-N-O-P spells.

The Gray Lady floats down slower, slower than she ever did. I look long into her face until she gives up and recedes. I sense I have begun the defeat of her when I resist giving her myself to react against.

— Gray Lady, you will not be needing to come again after now. I needed someone just like you. I breathed life into you when I was truly small and overpowered. I breathed the air of infant rage into a mean, big, tough gray lady who was mean in a way I never thought of no Not-Me.

And I made you so huge that I found you frightening, forgetting who it was made you. I created you, Gray Lady, and I banish you now to nothing as thin as the air of my infant rage.

My anger is now my ally. My life force claims all of me and cannot agree to lend you anymore. You are air to air I bury you back again.

I begin to feel the new moist skin overgrow the tough dried up scar tissues afterburns healing, healing the sunlight penetrating deeper, deeper into me, into my writing, into my descent in order to ascend with some tribute worth bearing, taking nothing on demand this giving, giving, giving away of me.

On a merciful current that flows in mercy I lay me down until I can sense the current flow in me. I open my eyes and I see things! Places, splendor I quake before and I create a voice to shout in joy and awe and belief and pain. And I wait and wait standing ready when there is no light to make me learn by. And a word floats by and I take hold of it and travel with it beyond the space, beyond the boundaries, beyond the unplanned uncharted inscape.

Healing and healing I begin to know myself in new shades of light.

The Gray Lady I hold up to air, and the next wind carries off the cobweb remains of her and with her, the remains of anyone that keeps me from my essential knowing.

I don't sense her around anywhere aboard this singular journey on this light wing, with no substance to speak of, and no more than this fragile, indomitable raybeam spirit of the path, where you pay for your share of the ride, at that.

I get on at least forever.

❧

There are two Jerusalems.

The one before us and the one we yearn for. At the end of our palms, at the end of our minds. At the end of exile. A place on earth where Heaven will prevail.

For years we had imagined both. Now we are here for the first time and the two images come together. The Kotel, the holy places, the sweet land oozing with history, the faces of people who kiss her stones. And from these, the longing arises in greater intensity.

And in our longing the rebuilt Jerusalem lives.

Jerusalem is a place in which to grieve. Grieving for what has been lost. Helps us to yearn for the future. Thus, the grieving in Jerusalem is redemptive.

I have been utterly self-centered. Completely taken up with my lost son, my lost dreams. Here, in Jerusalem the rungs of my awareness expand. The power of these words strike me: May God comfort you among the mourners for Zion and Jerusalem.

Here, I gain a context for a grief-stricken mother. Here I am with Rachel, Mother of Israel. And all the Rachels who have lost sons. Here I am waiting waiting for the promised return of sons to Jerusalem. The promised return of the Shechinah.

My posture changes. My heart expands beyond its pain. My hands reach out again to others who are broken.

I pray on an ocean of longing. I rise on a tide of hope.

Jerusalem

We make a sudden decision to take our first trip to Israel. I am packing. I am making decisions about what to leave and what to take. I wonder if there are parts of me and parts of my grief that will stay behind.

I reach into the drawer in the hall dresser for a pair of winter gloves I thought I had put there.

Inside the drawer
The tefillin
Lay in their velvet bag.
They are drawn taut
Around an empty center
They are empty of the head and hand
Empty of the heart
That filled them and shaped them.
Now their spirals turn inward inward.
How many lives
Have the long black wraps bound

And released.
Bound and released.

Until now, we were going to go to Jerusalem and now we are going to Jerusalem. In order to leave the children and my home and the setting for my grieving I suspend myself. Through the airplane window I see myself drawn like a translucent cloud against the blue-black sky over an ocean I have never crossed. I leave my continuity with my cloud woman and I keep only the moment I am recording.

The plane stops in London in the early morning. Two minyanim form, one Sefardi and one Ashkenazi.

The Sefardi reader takes longer, he lets the words linger lovingly on his lips, he releases them reluctantly.

— *Chazak baruch*! Be strong and blessed! The Sefardim are finished. A mother offers her eight small children breakfast of homemade bread. A *chassid* recites psalms in the dawn of the fourth day. He holds the book open with his hands while his eyes look beyond the room. His mouth hungrily bites the words from the air.

In each of us there is the hunger that makes us seek a source outside ourself. The hungry child who waits and receives nourishment provides a model by which we know our primary need; a point from which we begin to reach outward toward connectedness. The outreach develops. It is many-sided. It leads ultimately upward toward the primary relationship, person-to-God. It knows itself from inside itself in the hungry child who waits to receive.

The first night in Jerusalem I dream of a door.

It is copper and stone. The copper is beaten, intricate and beautiful. It is rarified with age. It bears the mark of its craftsman.

I awaken. I pray the first prayer of the first day on the balcony overlooking Jerusalem.

> *Work me*
> *Shape me*
> *Transform me.*
> *Take the raw grief*
> *And make of me an entry*
> *To take me beyond myself*
> *Let me bear*
> *The markings of Your Hand.*
> *Let the created*
> *Sense in herself the Creator.*
> *Teach me to wait*
> *With the faith*
> *Of the child within me*
> *Who waits to receive.*

To go to the Kotel, the Western Wall, we turn down the tour, turn down offers of taxis, turn down a map. We will walk together. We will find our way there. But walking there doesn't seem like enough. I want the preparation to be worthy of the tribute.

Something swells within me. The internal dialogue bursts forth. Do you hear? The Wall. I am going! I hug the words and embrace the sound and sense of the words inside my mind. It is one mile away...In the end my impatience is the appropriate tribute.

I have utterly lost patience for my eyes. Until now, never having experienced the Wall, I have been submerged in perceptual head turning. I have been subjugated by my mind. Now near the Wall, as never before, I am driven by another master. It is my soul. I feel it. I follow it as it leads me to the Wall. The brain is mindless in its perceptual scanning. The *neshamah*-soul suddenly throws figure and ground into dramatic reversal. The foreground is secondary; what you cannot see is primary. Now see.

I look and look and this new awareness floods and fills my field of vision until I see nothing at all. I begin to engage myself. I begin to know myself in integration as never before. I know my differentiation as never before. I see my brain/heart/mind. I sense my spiritual organs as easily as I feel my hand. I am drunk with this dance of myself. I lift my face. I make of me my prayer.

My tears fly to the Wall. The Wall wants my tears. I lay my cheek against the stone and listen.

I stand Wall-like and wait.

I begin to feel that I am not holding myself up but that the Wall holds me, like the Holy Ark which held its bearers.[25] I am held in the arms of a timeless Father Mother. Held beyond myself, I see I am a grown child and I am being forged and joined, cleaved back to my true axis point.

I have the sensation of having drunk in the wall through my lips.

My deepest thirst is satisfied. I weep the paradoxical tears of joy, tears for the thing so missing that is now in hand.

Suddenly my *neshamah*-soul is still, utterly still.

At the Wall I enter a new perspective. I fit into a frame that is wide enough to hold my grief. At the Wall, as never before, I am aware of loss. I am defined by what I lack. We are those who mourn Zion and Jerusalem. Here we are countrymen. Grief is our citizenship. Our status is designated by what we are bereft of. Relationship. Connectedness. Through the one generic loss I come to know mine in new light.

> *I write names on little papers.*
> *Little papers catch a prayer.*
> *They create a visible prayer.*
> *I close my eyes*
> *And feel the letters*
> *Resist the page.*
> *I feel the letters twist*
> *and pull themselves into the current.*
> *Up, up meet an energy*
> *that God sends down.*
> *Meeting it, the letters diffuse*
> *And break up into their original elements.*
> *They return to the fire*
> *Where they first were forged.*
> *Now they send out strands of energy.*
> *One to life,*
> *One to heal,*
> *One to make live.*
> *They ascend in order to descend.*

From my paper prayers
Down to their elements
Up to God,
And down to save!
Lift!
Send!
Heal!
Heal me, my man, my daughters.
Send us up, lower the power,
Mingle in us, heal us,
Fix us we are broken.
Reshape us into a new entity
In which we might sense wholeness.

Later in the same day, I return to the Kotel for *minchah*. The prayers stand in sharp relief; between these peaks lies the time in between. My *neshamah*-soul is still ordering priorities.

It is raining. I balance my prayer book and my umbrella. Out of the corner of my eye I see two ten-year-old girls skipping toward the Wall, carefree and playful, their long braids swinging against their shoulders. Suddenly one fades from my line of vision and one approaches. She takes three steps back and three forward and bends into prayer, her entire being suffused with pleading. She is as wholly immersed in the prayer as she was a moment ago wholly immersed in play.

I look at her face. Is this a child's face, twisted and contorted in pain and purpose, longing and straining in the direction of her longing?

My *neshamah*-think tells me that there are no old women or young girls in Jerusalem. There are only *neshamot*. Faces serve as disguises, and in Jerusalem disguises are thin. After my wet *minchah* prayer, I sit on a bench under my umbrella. I watch a few people climb down from the bus and approach the Wall. Heavy steps, burdened hearts. Then they face the Wall to pray. When they leave, they are changed. They exchange their faces at the Wall. They hang up the old ones and take new ones. Refreshed, they climb back up the hill to the bus to ride home.

In this city where the Soul has foothold and humanity is a quick-change artist, my pain is both more mellow and more acute.

At dinner in the hotel a slim, short, brown-haired American boy asks us if we've had dessert and if so, can we tell him what's good? I cry for my tall beautiful son. I cry for the demands made on him because he did not resemble the half-grown boy that was still inside him. I miss my beautiful son more in Jerusalem where everything is more. In Jerusalem it is more to have a son, more to appreciate the promise in a son, more to have, more to lose, more loss than I even knew to know him, and lose him. I ache seeing this Jerusalem he will never see.

Into the Jerusalem night I cry, where are you Yosef? Where? Is there Jerusalem beyond the pain and within the promise?

In Jerusalem far is near and beyond is possible. The eternal city plays havoc with my primitive notions of time and space. In Jerusalem, a wall mends my mental construction. It melts the hard edges of ordinary reality, of linear tie and causality. It offers me a fortress, a perspective that encompasses me, a reality both transcendent and communal.

In Jerusalem, I make the acquaintance of my soul. It leads me to a wall. Together we find in it the entrance that takes me beyond myself.

⁖

Chanukah.

The anniversary of my father's death. Yosef is named for him. Yosef who bears his name and some quality of spirit reminiscent of my father is a consolation for his loss. Now they are both gone.

Pain cuts a deeper path than I have ever known.

I see how tarnished the menorah is. I polish it rather listlessly. My hands seem to move through water, against resistance. I remember how we always dance with the children after the lighting. The memory saddens me because I cannot imagine reentering that easy joy.

I see two pairs of feet dancing together. Just the feet. I want to enter that dance. I whirl with them. For one wild moment I break out of my grief.

I hardly recognize my old spirits.

They are together. They are together. I weave through a dance with the dead. In that moment Heaven bends and earth reaches.

We touch.

All my memories of my father are safe.

All my experiences of Yosef are intact.

They are brothers now. Twin possibilities. For memory. For love. For reunion. For a dance that starts in my head and encircles my heart.

The wild dance breaks up grief only for a moment. But it is a beginning.

Grief has lost its stronghold.

Chanukah

It is customary to light the lights of Chanukah near a doorway or window in order to make known the miracle of Chanukah...[26]

Chanukah approaches. I prepare the menorah for its place in front of the big window, the one facing the street. I polish it, removing its light gray coat, revealing its hard, smooth glow. It is ready, this receptacle for mitzvah, this lantern that swings its light back onto history, back to the original Chanukah and forward into the present, where we stand before its lights, the pathway into time and space beyond us.

The menorah stands ready for its enactment of dedication. And I?

I look out at the tree that stands before the window. I stare into its bare branches, wondering what secrets it has to tell. In the wintry wind, its branches flail and scrape against the glass delivering an insistent message, I cannot cipher, in a strange interplay of hoarse shriek and gentle whisper. I hear you, I hear you, Tree. My attempt to soothe yields only a more determined cry. I escape the room.

I busy myself with daily chores. This activity raises my spirit for a while and clears my head which turns inevitably back to its issues.

— I am doubly burdened, I hear myself say.

— Whom or what do I address? Chanukah, I answer:

— On Chanukah he will die again. This is the floodgate that releases my tears and flow of my mind:

— Yosef ben Judith my father died nineteen years ago, on the third light of Chanukah twenty-two months before my son Yosef ben Judith was born who died four months before Chanukah his seventeenth birthday.

> I am over my head nineteen,
> Twenty-two, three, four, two,
> And seventeen times.
> I traverse the entire globe
> In double circumference, times two.
> When I land, I am on the floor.
> I am huddled down hugging gravity.
> My face is hidden.
> My burdens weigh me down,
> They pull me and my shoulders
> Downward, downward.
> I carry them.

All of them,

All of All of them

For All of them.

The wo/man

sonless   orphaned

widowered   manless

childless   motherless

Wrapped, huddled close

In the space of my arms

Upon my shoulders,

Down, down through the Ages.

Too weighed down to walk upright,

We are down here. Here!

DON'T LOOK.

Whoever looks will see too much.

The first one who looks will Know,

And will feel ashamed on the outside,

And will be pulled onto the inside.

DON'T LOOK AWAY.

For if no one looks at us,

If we see no one seeing us,

How will we know ourselves?

I stay for minutes or centuries

Saturated with the Every and All burdened bereft.

Stay! stay, they call to me.

Stay with us,

Believe in us, confirm us.

When I rise over myself
I neither stay nor abandon
The All-of-One and One-Of-All
Person of grief.
I am not him
But I am of him.
I am not inside her skin
But I am sent by her.
I do not cry their tears
But my own, that taste of theirs.
In the largesse of my arms cradling me
My father and my son are inextricably
Bound close to me to this recreated self
For they influence the code of its genesis
As they never did before.
I have them woven into the warp of my mind
They are loomed into my consciousness
The threads of them spin bright,
Steady, and inevitable.
There they created me again
As never before I create them creating me
In creating myself endlessly as never before.
As never before, they are close to each other
As they never were before.
They are brothers now,
Equivalent potentialities
Presenting face to face

The alternate openings
Onto the past and the future.

I feel the fresh new skin of my awareness. I walk self-consciously inside it. I approach the window. There the tree still speaks in its shrieks and whispers. I speak to the tree:

— What secrets of time do you keep buried beneath your winter face, old ancient one? You flail all through the winter sky searching for spring when all the while the seeds for your own rebirth are within you.

— Here, I soothe, I have given you the merit of the menorah standing before you.

The menorah stands ready.
It is faithful,
It waits and seeks its moment
To transcend itself and time
In its holy purpose.
It stands ready before the window
An opening onto the pathways
Of all our journeys.
Welcome.
Come in, it calls
To openings that open
Onto the portals of openings
That go on opening,
That spill open the Light
Flowing forward,

Drawing forth the incandescent,
Moonbeam pathways
To Infinity-Ain Sof.
Onto this opening I enter alone.
My soul knows the way.

The Gift

A woman I have never met calls me. Her sixteen-year-old son died in a skiing accident.

She calls me during the Awful Months to share with me the most helpful comment made to her during her Awful Months. She says, "Your son brought you many gifts during his life. He will continue to bring you gifts after his death."

After her call, at some point during the Awful Months, I find myself trying out this perspective. Any gift of love that we share as a family or among our friends, I rename as a gift from Yosef. Any new awareness, our need for escape into comic antics, even these I attribute to Yosef.

It helps me to have Yosef, the object of our crushing pain and sorrow and shock, assume a role in the healing and in the recovery.

How would Yosef feel about this? Yosef had a way of staying somewhat hidden, somewhat mysterious. He kept his own counsel. He enjoyed moving behind veils to make things happen.

I imagine myself asking Yosef what he thinks of this idea. I imagine him answering me with his impish grin: No one knows for sure Mom, but why not go with the idea?

And now, my Thread of Blue, my widened boundaries, the frame I have in which to receive the pain and losses of others, the acceptance I have gained, the sense of process, the dying and living again. All these belong in the gifts he still gives us.

I feel strengthened by the words of the other mother. These words too become a part of Yosef's gift, a part of the stream I can follow back to its source.

And then I recall that the other mother's words are a part of her gift that came to her at the death of her son. Soon, I begin to see that there is a circle and it is wider than I knew. It is wider and still wider until all we experience in the pain and in the privilege is still the gift. And all the layers of experience accumulate and grow and reflect one another like so many layers of translucent silk. And then we know we are in the heart of mankind and it beats in us.

It is said of the rare blue in the bibical Thread of Blue that its color is the blue of the ocean. The blue of the ocean is the blue of the sky, and the blue of the sky is a reflection of the Throne of God.[27] The Thread of Blue opens for me the horizon of the ocean, the realm of the Interpersonal. The Interpersonal, the hallowed human relationship, receives and reflects the Vertical, the Godly, the very Throne of Heaven.

The gift of the Thread of Blue is all the pain and all the privilege we can find in living.

It is a rare gift.

Afterword

A stranger offers me the most healing gift: She offers me a way to find Yosef in the continuing unfolding of our family. She gives me a gift of the heart. Because she too has lost a son, her gift is believable. I know how it was forged out of her tears and the wisdom that grew in her heart.

Since that time, people continue to offer me gifts. People who have read *Thread of Blue* and who tell me they have let it change them. People who dare to pay a *shivah* call and sit in silence in tribute to a great loss. People who have used this small book to heal, to help others heal. People who have used this small book as a guide to one heart seeking Hashem.

All these gifts belong in the gifts Yosef gave us.

Notes

1. Numbers 15:38
2. Chazon Ish, A. Y. Karelitz, *Collected Writings*
3. Genesis 47:29
4. Leviticus 21:1
5. Jonah 2:3
6. *Avot* 4:16
7. *Shabbat* 88b
8. Proverbs 20:27
9. *Megillah* 7b
10. Deuteronomy 28:9; *Shabbat* 133b
11. Job 19:26
12. Ibn Ezra on Isaiah 54
13. Jeremiah 31:14
14. Genesis 12:1
15. Ramban on Genesis 12:6
16. *Shabbat* 152b
17. Proverbs 27:19
18. *Berachot* 5b
19. *Pachad Yitzchak*, Yom Kippur 19:8
20. *Rosh Hashanah prayer book*
21. Hosea 14:2
22. Rashi on Genesis 18:2
23. *Zohar, Terumah* 161
24. *Avot* 4:16
25. Joshua 4:18
26. Rambam, *Laws of Chanukah* 4:7
27. Rashi on *Menachot* 43b

Glossary

ahavah — love

Av — fifth month of the Jewish year as counted from Nissan

ba'alei teshuvah — those who return to the Tradition

brit milah — circumcision

Chanukah — Festival of lights

Elul — sixth month of the Jewish year as counted from Nissan

kavod — honor

Kaddish — memorial prayer for the dead

menorah — candelabrum used on Chanukah

minchah — afternoon prayers

minyan — prayer quorum

mitzvah/mitzvot — commandment/s

neshamah/neshamot — soul/ s

rachamim — compassion

rachum — compassionate

Rebbe — teacher

Rosh Hashanah — the New Year

shacharit — morning prayers

shivah — week of mourning

simchah — joy

Simchat Torah — festival celebrating the renewed cycle of the Torah

Sukkot — festival of Tabernacles

tallit — four-cornered prayer shawl

tefillah — prayer

tefillin — prayer phylacteries

Tishrei — seventh month of the Jewish year as counted from Nissan

yisurim — trials

zivug — mate